VIRTUAL HISTORY TOURS

Look around an

EGYPTIAN TOMB

Liz Gogerly

ARCTURUS

This edition first published by Arcturus Publishing
Distributed by Black Rabbit Books
123 South Broad Street
Mankato
Minnesota MN 56001

Copyright © 2008 Arcturus Publishing Limited

Printed in China

Library of Congress Cataloging-in-Publication Data
Gogerly, Liz.
  Look around an Egyptian tomb : by Liz Gogerly.
      p. cm. -- (Virtual history tours)
Includes index.
ISBN 978-1-84193-719-9 (alk. paper)
1. Tutankhamen, King of Egypt--Tomb--Juvenile literature.
2. Tombs--Egypt--Juvenile literature.
3. Funeral rites and ceremonies--Egypt--Juvenile literature.
4. Egypt--Antiquities--Juvenile literature. I. Title.

DT87.5.G64 2007
932--dc22

              2007007982

9 8 7 6 5 4 3 2

Series concept: Alex Woolf
Editor: Jenni Rainford
Designer: Ian Winton
Plan artwork: Phil Gleaves

Picture credits:
Art Archive: 10 (Dagli Orti), 16 (Egyptian Museum Turin / Dagli Orti), 20 (Pharaonic Village Cairo / Dagli Orti), 21 (Egyptian Museum Cairo / Dagli Orti), 22 (Egyptian Museum Cairo / Dagli Orti), 24 (Egyptian Museum Turin / Dagli Orti), 27 (Musée du Louvre Paris / Dagli Orti), 28 (Dagli Orti)
Bridgeman Art Library: 14 (The Illustrated London News Picture Library, London, UK)
Corbis: 4 (Royalty-Free), 6 (Bettmann), 7 (Sandro Viannini), 8 (Sandro Viannini), 9 (Carmen Redondo), 13 (Royalty-Free), 15 (Gianni Dagli Orti), 17 (Gianni Dagli Orti), 18 (Hulton-Deutsch Collection), 19 (Royalty-Free), 23 (Supreme Council of Antiquities / epa), 25 (Bowers Museum of Cultural Art), 26 (Sandro Viannini), 29 (Christie's Images)
TopFoto: 11 (Topham PicturePoint)
Arcturus Publishing Ltd: 12

CONTENTS

The Tomb of Tutankhamen 4

The Hidden Stairway 6

The Corridor Beyond 8

The Antechamber 10

The Guardian Statues 12

The Annex 14

Items for the Afterlife 16

The Burial Chamber 18

The Sarcophagus and Coffins 20

The Golden Mask and Mummy 22

The Treasury 24

The Canopic Shrine 26

The Anubis Shrine 28

Timeline 30

Glossary and Further Information 31

Index 32

THE TOMB OF TUTANKHAMEN

Step into the mysterious Valley of the Kings in Egypt. All around you are limestone hills. It's a dry, barren place, and nobody lives here. Carved into the stone beneath your feet are the tombs of pharaohs, the rulers of ancient Egypt, such as Rameses VI, as well as members of the royal family. You'll see a simple doorway leading to the famous, treasure-filled tomb of the young pharaoh Tutankhamen.

TUTANKHAMEN: SEE PAGE 7

The Valley of the Kings

The Valley of the Kings is in the Theban Hills on the west bank of the River Nile. Its Arabic name is *Biban el Moluk*, which means "Doors of the Kings." In ancient times, the pharaohs of the New Kingdom (1550–1070 BCE) made the city of Luxor, on the east side of the Nile, their capital. The pharaohs wanted to be buried in a secret place instead of the pyramids of the Old Kingdom, so they chose the limestone hills on the west side of the Nile.

The final resting place of Tutankhamen lies in the Valley of the Kings.

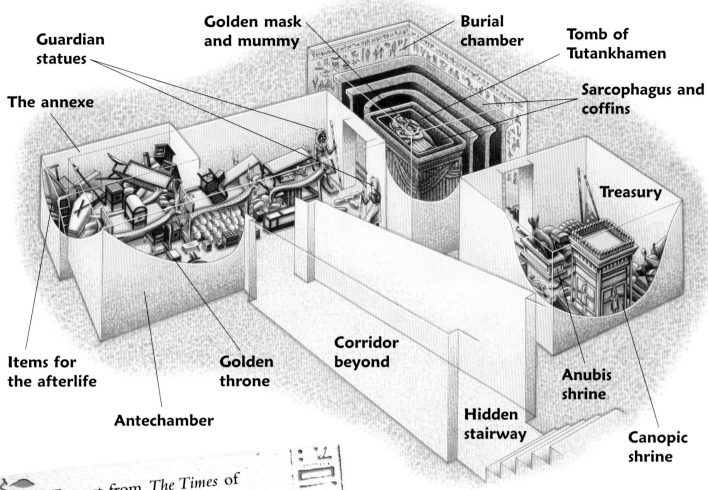

Guardian statues

Golden mask and mummy

Burial chamber

Tomb of Tutankhamen

The annexe

Sarcophagus and coffins

Treasury

Items for the afterlife

Golden throne

Corridor beyond

Anubis shrine

Antechamber

Hidden stairway

Canopic shrine

Amazing discovery

Sixty-two tombs have been found in the Valley of the Kings. English Egyptologist Howard Carter discovered the Tutankhamen's tomb on November 4, 1922. Carter's work was funded by Lord Carnarvon, and the two men had been searching for this tomb since 1917. Near the end of 1922, Carter and Carnarvon were thinking of giving up. Lord Carnarvon was back in England when Carter discovered the tomb's entrance. Carter sent him a telegram: "At last have made wonderful discovery in Valley. A magnificent tomb with seals intact, closed up until your arrival; congratulations!"

5

THE HIDDEN STAIRWAY

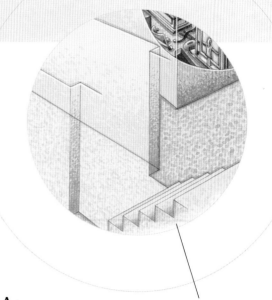

The hidden stairway

Look down the stairway at the entrance to the tomb. You can count 12 steps, each one carved into the rock more than 3,000 years ago. Though it's dark, the stairway feels roomier than you might expect—it's about 10 feet (3 m) high and 6 feet (1.8 m) wide. But how would you get a great stone sarcophagus down these stairs? At the bottom of the steps is another sealed doorway.

Secret tombs for the pharaohs

In ancient Egypt, the pharaohs were buried in special tombs. Their bodies were mummified (wrapped in cloth) and laid to rest in a coffin or mummy case. The coffin was placed in a large stone sarcophagus, which was taken to the burial chamber inside the tomb. Also buried with the pharaoh were treasures and things he would need in the afterlife, such as furniture, food, fine jewels, clothes, statues, and boats. Such items were tempting to tomb robbers.

AFTERLIFE: SEE PAGE 16

Treasures from Tutankhamen's tomb came out the same way they went in—via the secret stairway.

Beating the tomb robbers

The pharaohs of the Old Kingdom (2690–2180 BCE) built enormous tombs called pyramids. But they were easy to find and so were often robbed. The pharaohs of the New Kingdom (1550–1070 BCE) built their tombs underground, making it more difficult for the robbers to steal from these secret tombs.

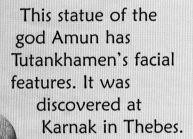

This statue of the god Amun has Tutankhamen's facial features. It was discovered at Karnak in Thebes.

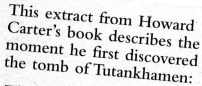

This extract from Howard Carter's book describes the moment he first discovered the tomb of Tutankhamen:

There was always the horrible possibility . . . that the tomb was unfinished, never completed and never used: if it had been finished there was the depressing probability that it had been completely plundered in ancient times. On the other hand, there was just the chance of an untouched or only partially plundered tomb, and it was with ill-suppressed excitement that I watched the descending steps of the staircase, as one by one they came to light.

Howard Carter,
The Tomb of Tutankhamen
(National Geographic Adventure Classics, 2003)

Who was Tutankhamen?

Not much is known about the life of Tutankhamen. He was possibly the son-in-law of the pharaoh Akhenaten (ruled 1352–1336 BCE). In 1336 BCE, Tutankhamen became pharaoh even though he was just nine years old. He was too young to rule alone, so major decisions were made by Ay, a relative of Tutankhamen, and a general, Horemheb. During Tutankhamen's short reign, the religion of ancient Egypt was changed back to worshipping many gods. Unfortunately, Tutankhamen died young, possibly when he was about 19.

DEATH OF TUTANKHAMEN: SEE PAGE 23

THE CORRIDOR BEYOND

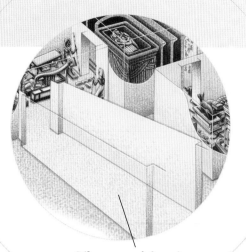

The corridor beyond the stairway

Look closer at the doorway at the bottom of the stairs. You'll see that it's covered in stamps (or impressions) from large oval seals. Each seal contains tiny pictures that represent words in ancient Egyptian. Near the bottom of the door, the pictures on the seals spell out the name of a king: Tut-ankh-Amen. The name is surrounded by an oval border, known as a cartouche.

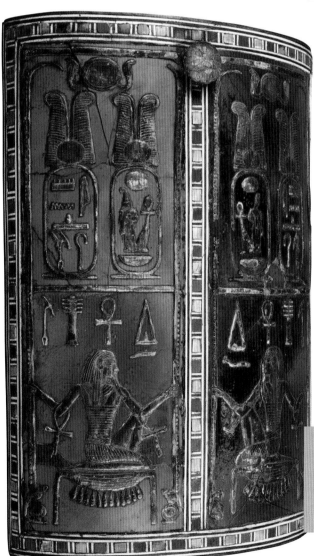

Tomb robbers

When Carter and his men chipped away at the plaster door at the bottom of the stairs, they could see a corridor beyond. The rubble that filled in the top left-hand side of the door and the limestone chippings on the corridor floor told Carter that the tomb had probably been robbed in ancient times. Carter knew all too well that recent archaeologists had discovered many tombs that had been wrecked and plundered by thieves thousands of years ago.

This beautiful jewelry chest was just the kind of treasure robbers looked for when stealing from the pharaohs' tombs.

What's in a seal?

Within Tutankhamen's tomb were four doors that were blocked and covered with plaster. The plaster was stamped using large oval seals. Some larger seals are requests to the gods to protect the pharaoh's resting place. Other seals spell out Tutankhamen's name. There are also many smaller seals that were probably made using signet rings belonging to the officials who were present at the sealing of the tomb.

This is the seal of Rameses II. Each ancient Egyptian ruler had his own seal.

This extract from Howard Carter's book describes the moment he found a seal representing the pharaoh Tutankhamen.

On the lower part [of the door] the seal impressions were much clearer, and we were able without any difficulty to make out on several of them the name of Tut-ankh-Amen. This added enormously to the interest of the discovery. If we had found, as seemed certain, the tomb of the shadowy monarch, whose tenure of the throne coincided with one of the most interesting periods of the whole of Egyptian history, we should indeed have reason to congratulate ourselves.

Howard Carter,
The Tomb of Tutankhamen

Lost in translation

Each seal impression is made up of the ancient Egyptian picture writing called hieroglyphs. Translating hieroglyphs into English is not an easy job. Howard Carter and Lord Carnarvon had two experts with them to help them read the ancient text.

CARTER'S TEAM: SEE PAGES 10

9

THE ANTECHAMBER

At the end of the corridor, through another seal-covered door, is the antechamber. This room measures about 25 feet (7.62 m) by 11 feet (3.4 m). Its walls are covered with white plaster. You gasp with wonder. Everywhere you look you see treasure and the sparkle of gold! Lining one wall are three enormous golden couches, carved to look like strange creatures. Scattered around the room are boxes, caskets, chairs, and vases, all gold or painted with beautiful patterns.

The antechamber

This 20th-century painting shows Howard Carter discovering the antechamber for the first time.

A quick burial

The tomb of Tutankhamen was much smaller than other royal tombs found in the Valley of the Kings. Carter and his team believed that these underground rooms had not been planned as a pharaoh's tomb. This, and other evidence found later, made them think that Tutankhamen had been buried in a hurry.

BURIALS: SEE PAGE 14

Religion

Religion was very important to the ancient Egyptians. Many of the objects found in the royal tombs represented different gods. Within Tutankhamen's tomb, the great gilt couches in the antechamber were funerary beds. They were probably used for special rituals when the body of Tutankhamen was being prepared for burial.

A close-up of the lion goddess Mehet from one of the corners of the gilt couch found near the guardian statues.

Here Howard Carter recalls the wonderful moment when he first saw some of the treasures in the antechamber:

Let the reader imagine how the objects appeared to us as we looked down upon them from our spyhole in the blocked doorway, casting the beam of light from our torch—the first light that had pierced the darkness of the chamber for three thousand years—from one group of objects to another, in a vain attempt to interpret the treasure that lay before us. The effect was bewildering, overwhelming. . . .

Howard Carter,
The Tomb of Tutankhamen

Animal couches

One of the couches in Tutankhamen's tomb looked like a lion and represented the goddess Mehet, who was responsible for flooding the Nile. Another couch was part crocodile, part lion, and part hippopotamus and represented Ammut, the goddess also known as the Devourer of the Dead. The third couch represented the cow goddess, Mehet-Weret. She was responsible for raising Tutankhamen to join the sun god in the afterlife.

11

THE GUARDIAN STATUES

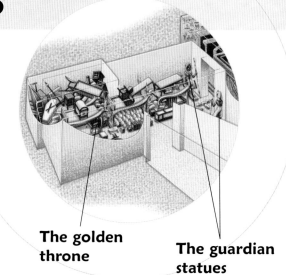

The golden throne

The guardian statues

Peer through the darkness to the northeast corner of the antechamber. To either side of another sealed entrance stand two life-size statues of Tutankhamen. They are made of wood and covered in black resin. Their wigs, loincloths, and sandals are gold plated. The statues are facing each other, as though guarding the doorway. Hidden under the animal couch is a beautiful golden throne. On the back is a picture of Tutankhamen with his wife, Ankhesenamen.

The Afterlife

The ancient Egyptians believed that the dead went on living in the next world, which was known as the afterlife. To plan for a king's afterlife, his body had to be prepared and protected. Tutankhamen's body was preserved by a process called mummification.

BURIAL ARTEFACTS:
SEE PAGES 14-17

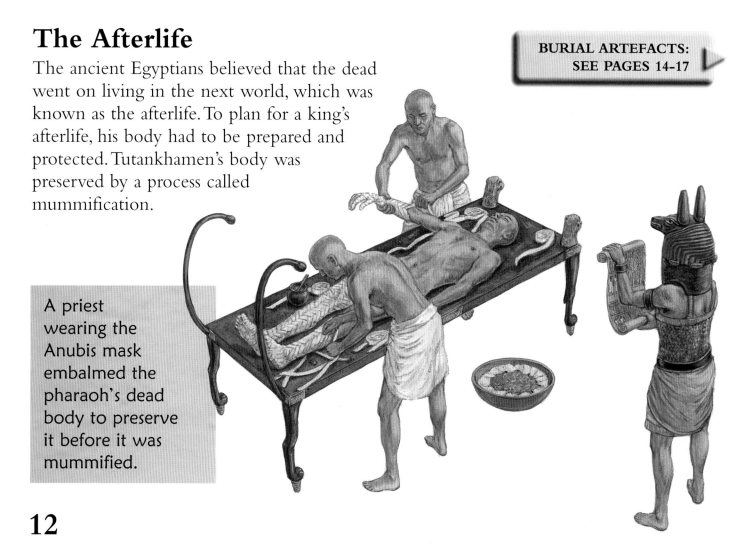

A priest wearing the Anubis mask embalmed the pharaoh's dead body to preserve it before it was mummified.

12

Making a mummy

At the start of the mummification process, some of Tutankhamen's body parts were removed, embalmed, and carefully laid to rest. The pharaoh had to be buried with all kinds of things he would need in the next life, such as treasures, food, and fine jewels.

MUMMIFICATION:
SEE PAGES 26-29

A scene from the back of the golden throne shows Tutankhamen with his young wife, Ankhesenamen.

Here Howard Carter describes the golden throne:

Below this couch stood another of the great artistic treasures of the tomb—perhaps the greatest so far taken out—a throne, overlaid with gold from top to bottom, and richly adorned with glass, faience, and stone inlay. . . . It was the panel of the back, however, that was the chief glory of the throne, and I have no hesitation in claiming for it that it is the most beautiful thing that has yet been found in Egypt.

Howard Carter,
The Tomb of Tutankhamen

Tutankhamen's statues

The statues of Tutankhamen are 5.6 feet (1.7 m) tall. Howard Carter described them as "strange and imposing." Carter also said that the statues looked like sentinels (guards) that were protecting the entrance to the burial chamber. In fact, the statues represented Tutankhamen's *ka* (soul or spirit). The ancient Egyptians believed that the spirit of a dead pharaoh lived on in the *ka* statue.

THE ANNEX

The annexe

Hidden away in the southern corner of the antechamber, under the funerary couch, is another door. Beyond this door is a chamber that Howard Carter called the annex. It's the smallest room in the tomb, measuring just over 13 feet (4 m) by 7.9 feet (2.4 m). Despite its size, it contains more objects than any other chamber. However, tomb robbers have left the room in chaos. Countless objects are heaped together in huge piles, some reaching over 5.9 feet (1.8 m) high.

A bed fit for a king

Among the clutter were four beds that Carter believed were actually used by Tutankhamen in his lifetime. They were placed here for his use in the afterlife. The legs of each bed were shaped like a cat's legs, and the most striking bed had a golden footboard and a linen-mesh mattress. This was comfort indeed in ancient Egypt—ordinary people slept on mats on the floor. One of the most interesting beds was Tutankhamen's roll-away bed—it folded away cleverly—the only one of its kind to have been found in ancient Egypt.

Carter and his team carefully removed the royal beds from Tutankhamen's tomb.

14

Beautiful headrests

Ancient Egyptians often used headrests to support their heads while they slept. The headrests were usually decorated with gods and goddesses for protection while sleeping. These headrests were also buried in the tombs of pharaohs.

This ivory headrest from ancient Egypt may have been covered with soft material to make it more comfortable.

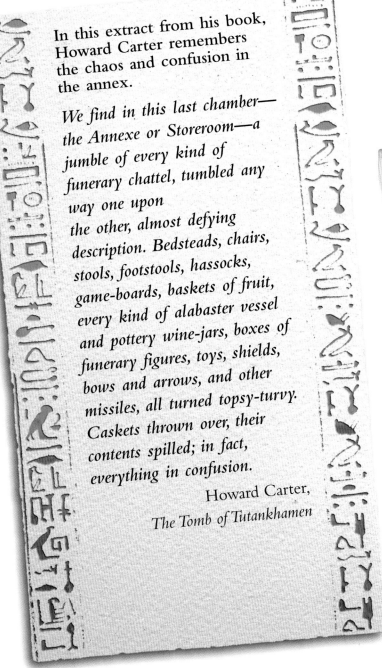

In this extract from his book, Howard Carter remembers the chaos and confusion in the annex.

We find in this last chamber— the Annexe or Storeroom—a jumble of every kind of funerary chattel, tumbled any way one upon the other, almost defying description. Bedsteads, chairs, stools, footstools, hassocks, game-boards, baskets of fruit, every kind of alabaster vessel and pottery wine-jars, boxes of funerary figures, toys, shields, bows and arrows, and other missiles, all turned topsy-turvy. Caskets thrown over, their contents spilled; in fact, everything in confusion.

Howard Carter,
The Tomb of Tutankhamen

The king's headrests

In Tutankhamen's annex, there were four headrests: two made from ivory, another made from turquoise glass, and another made from dark blue faience (a glass-type material). Each headrest was engraved with Tutankhamen's name. One of the ivory headrests showed Shu, the god of the air, holding up the heavens. Two lions sat beside him to protect the horizon. One faced the east and the other, the west.

ITEMS FOR THE AFTERLIFE

The annexe

On the floor of the annex you'll see baskets, pots, vases, urns, cups, and goblets scattered everywhere. Hidden under a pile of boxes is a vase decorated with a boat and two figures. It would once have contained oils, perfume, or cosmetics. On top of the vase is the upturned base of a game board. In a white box, there's a secret store of hunting sticks that look like large boomerangs. On the lid of the box, you'll see some dirty footprints. Quite possibly, they belonged to the tomb robbers all those years ago!

Food for the future

The pharaoh needed with him in the afterlife all the things he used in his daily life—food, drink, clothing, and cosmetics. The annex in Tutankhamen's tomb was filled with baskets containing different kinds of bread, seeds, fruit, nuts, and spices, as well as jars of wine. Archaeologists even found joints of meat in the tomb! These were placed inside special egg-shaped containers.

A selection of nuts, seeds, eggs, and fruits found within Tutankhamen's tomb, to feed him in the afterlife.

16

Entertainment for eternity

A pharaoh had to be kept amused in the afterlife. Tutankhamen was buried with games, musical instruments, weapons, and writing materials. Senet was a popular game in ancient Egypt, and four game boards were found in Tutankhamen's tomb.

Play the game

During the New Kingdom, the game of Senet had special religious importance. People believed a person's ability to play this game represented their passage to the afterlife.

A report from the *Daily Telegraph* of London:

The bows and arrows excited supreme interest. In design they are not unlike the conventional bow and arrow of modern times, but they display a remarkable ingenuity and thoroughness in construction. It was apparent that they had been placed in the tomb with Tutankhamen [sic] to assist his ancient Majesty in combating any enemies who might attempt to retard his progress from this world to the next.

Nicholas Reeves,
The Complete Tutankhamen: The King, the Tomb, the Treasure
(Thames and Hudson, 1995)

An ancient Egyptian wooden game of Senet. The small drawer contained the gaming pieces.

THE BURIAL CHAMBER

The sealed doorway in the antechamber has been chipped away. Once through the door, you enter the heart of the royal tomb—the burial chamber. In front of you is a gigantic golden shrine. The room measures just 23 feet (7 m) by 13 feet (4 m) and the shrine is so big, you can barely squeeze past it. The walls have been painted golden yellow, and the pictures tell the story of Tutankhamen's journey to the afterlife.

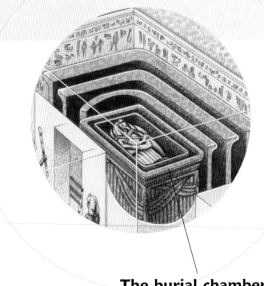

The burial chamber

Opening the shrines

Tutankhamen's burial chamber was opened by Howard Carter on February 17, 1923. First he pulled back the giant bolts and opened the heavy double doors of the golden shrine. Inside, there was a second smaller shrine, and he discovered two more shrines inside that.

THE BOOK OF THE DEAD: SEE PAGE 23

Howard Carter, A. R. Callender, and an Egyptian archaeologist worked together to open the doors of the shrine.

Shrine decoration

All the shrines were made of gilded wood (wood decorated with sheets of gold) and were covered in writing from the sacred books: the *Book of the Dead*, the *Book of the Heavenly Cow*, and the *Book of Amduat*. These books contained instructions, spells and prayers to help the king to reach the afterlife. The shrines were also decorated with pictures of Egyptian gods such as Isis and Anubis.

The burial chamber as it is today. The paintings on the west wall show 12 squatting baboon deities (gods).

The *Times* reports on the opening of Tutankhamen's tomb, February 1923:

The process of opening this doorway bearing the royal insignia and guarded by protective statues of the King had taken several hours of careful manipulation under the intense heat. It finally ended in a wonderful revelation, for before the spectators was the resplendent mausoleum of the King, a spacious, beautiful, decorated chamber, completely occupied by an immense shrine covered with gold inlaid with brilliant blue faience.

Jon E. Lewis, editor,
The Mammoth Book of How It Happened (Robinson, 1998)

Paintings on the walls

Many of the tombs found in the Valley of the Kings were beautifully decorated. By contrast, Tutankhamen's tomb was very simple. The burial chamber was the only room to have wall paintings, and these pictures were not very detailed. Many of the pictures had been spoiled by damp. However, it was possible to see scenes showing Tutankhamen embracing Osiris and the "Opening of the Mouth" ceremony. The small size of the room and the simple wall paintings has led historians to believe that Tutankhamen was buried in a hurry.

OPENING OF THE MOUTH CEREMONY: SEE PAGE 29

THE SARCOPHAGUS AND COFFINS

The golden doors of the fourth shrine open to reveal a stone sarcophagus. It measures about 8.9 feet (2.7 m) long by 4.9 feet (1.5 m) wide. Around the outside of the sarcophagus you can see the goddesses Neith, Nephthys, Selkis and Isis carved into the stone. They spread their wings around the corners as though protecting the coffins within.

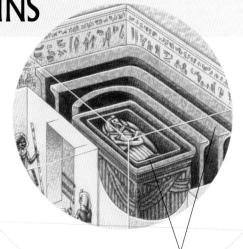

The sarcophagus and coffins

This is a reconstruction of Tutankhamen's coffins. There are two coffins inside this large wooden one. The mummy lies in the third coffin.

Lifting the lid

Beneath the heavy lid of the sarcophagus was a magnificent coffin shaped to contain a mummy. It was made of beautiful gilded wood and encrusted with glass and semi-precious stones. The coffin was made to look like Tutankhamen representing the god Osiris. There were two more coffins inside this one. The innermost coffin was made of solid gold, weighed 243 pounds (110 kg), and contained the mummy of the young king.

The golden coffins

Howard Carter had never expected to discover such elaborately decorated coffins. Each of them showed a different image of Tutankhamen. He was holding a scepter (a staff held by pharaohs) and flail (a tool used for threshing grain)—the symbols of his divine kingship.

The third coffin is made from beaten solid gold. The heavy lid can be raised using the two handles at the side.

Howard Carter on opening the sarcophagus:

With intense excitement I drew back the bolts of the last and unsealed doors; they slowly swung open, and there, filling the entire area within . . . stood an immense yellow quartzite sarcophagus, intact, with the lid still firmly fixed in its place, just as the pious hands had left it. It was certainly a thrilling moment, as we gazed upon the spectacle enhanced by the striking contrast—the glitter of metal— of the golden shrines shielding it.

Howard Carter,
The Tomb of Tutankhamen

Made to measure?

The second wooden coffin was the most beautifully decorated of the three. However, its face was the least like other portraits of Tutankhamen. This has led some historians to think that this coffin was not originally made for Tutankhamen. It is further evidence that the young king was buried very quickly.

TUTANKHAMEN'S DEATH:
SEE PAGE 23

THE GOLDEN MASK AND MUMMY

There are four small handles to lift the lid off the final coffin, or mummy case. Underneath the lid is a beautifully preserved mummy. The body is covered in black oils and wrapped in linen. Even so, you can still make out the glorious golden mask. His eyes are made from precious stones and they seem to look straight at you. Underneath the mask and outer trappings of the mummy is the preserved body of Tutankhamen. Wrapped inside the bandages are 150 jewels and amulets.

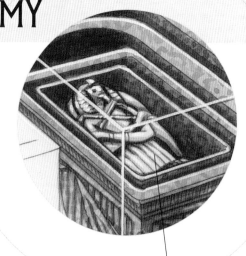

The golden mask and mummy

The trappings of the mummy

The mummy was covered with gold hands holding the scepter and flail as well as a gold collar decorated with gems and glass. Also found with the mummy was a mysterious necklace that had a scarab beetle made from yellow-green glass at its center. Recently, scientists discovered that the glass had been created when a meteorite hit the desert sand.

This golden death mask of Tutankhamen was made in the likeness of the pharaoh. This was so that he would recognize his body in the afterlife.

The Book of the Dead

In ancient Egypt, priests preparing a body followed the *Book of the Dead*. This gave detailed instructions on how to prepare the mummy and where to place jewels and amulets to help the king's passage to the afterlife.

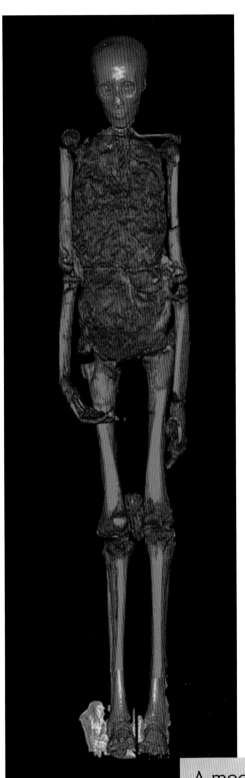

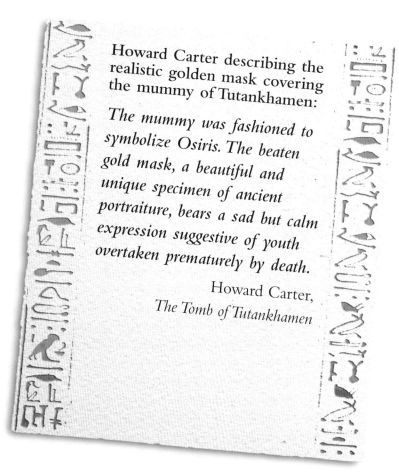

Howard Carter describing the realistic golden mask covering the mummy of Tutankhamen:

The mummy was fashioned to symbolize Osiris. The beaten gold mask, a beautiful and unique specimen of ancient portraiture, bears a sad but calm expression suggestive of youth overtaken prematurely by death.

Howard Carter,
The Tomb of Tutankhamen

The secrets of the mummy

The oils and resins used in the burial ceremony have damaged much of Tutankhamen's mummy. However, scientists have managed to discover more personal details about the king by studying his mummified remains. He was short, probably about 5 feet, 4 inches (1.6 m) tall. It is believed that he was about 19 when he died. Nobody knows how he died, but he was rather weak and had missing ribs and broken bones. Some people think he was murdered, though the truth may be less sinister. Perhaps the young king had an accident or a fall.

A modern CT scan of Tutankhamen's mummy reveals his skeleton in more detail.

THE TREASURY

The treasury

A small open door in the eastern wall of the burial chamber leads to the treasury. This room measures about 15.4 feet (4.7 m) by 12.5 feet (3.8 m) and is full of beautiful objects. You'll see model boats, a chariot, and a large gilded cow head representing the god Hathor. Throughout the room are boxes—some painted or decorated with jewels. The lids have already been moved—probably the work of tomb robbers!

Shabtis

In the northeast corner of the treasury sat 10 boxes containing *shabti* figures. These small models of people were made from wood, stone, or colored clay. They represented servants who worked on behalf of Tutankhamen in the afterlife. In total, 413 *shabtis* were found in the tomb— 365 of them were workmen, a servant for each day of the year. The *shabtis* were discovered with nearly 2,000 tiny tools, including picks, hoes, and baskets.

The ancient Egyptians believed that a magical spell brought the *shabti* figure to life to serve the dead.

Tutankhamen's children

In one simple wooden box lay two tiny coffins. Inside the coffins were the mummies of two baby girls. They were probably Tutankhamen's children who had died before or during birth.

Funeral boats

Model boats were commonly buried with pharaohs of the New Kingdom. In Tutankhamen's tomb there were 35 different boats, the largest measuring over 8 feet (2.5 m). These simple fishing boats or river-going boats, called skiffs, were placed in the tomb for the pharaoh to use on his journey to the afterlife.

Ancient Egyptians were often buried with model boats. Sometimes these were crewed by servants and oarsmen.

From chapter VI of the *Book of the Dead*, usually carved on the body of the *shabti*:

Oh shabti, listen to me. I have been called to render the various tasks the deceased spirits must carry out in the Netherworld, you must know shabti, that you with your tools must obey the man and fulfil his needs. It will be you, shabti, who will be punished instead of me by the guards of the Dwat (the world of the dead): you will sow the fields, fill the canals with water and move the sand from east to west. Your answer will always be: I am here, awaiting orders.

Aude Gros de Beler,
Tutankhamen
(Grange Books, 2004)

THE CANOPIC SHRINE

Pushed against the east wall of the treasury, you'll see the canopic shrine. Howard Carter said it was "so lovely that it made one gasp with wonder." It stands nearly 7 feet (2 m) tall and on each side of it are the golden figures of the goddesses Isis, Nephthys, Neith, and Selkis. Their bodies face into the shrine, and their arms are wide open. On top of

The canopic shrine

the shrine are rows of cobras made from colored glass. Inside this great chest are the embalmed body parts of Tutankhamen.

A view from one side of the canopic shrine. The goddess Selkis protects the king's body parts.

The embalming process

The body of the pharaoh had to be prepared for the afterlife. Embalming was a process that kept the corpse from decaying. There were special places called embalming workshops where this process was carried out.

EMBALMING WORKSHOPS:
SEE PAGE 28

Removing the organs

In the embalming workshops, the body was washed and shaved. Then the brain was removed using a hook inserted up the nose. Next, the liver, lungs, stomach, and intestines were taken away—only the pharaoh's heart was left in place! The parts were then dried, wrapped in linen, and placed in canopic jars to preserve them.

Embalmed body parts were often placed in canopic jars. This jar has a stopper in the form of the god Duamutef, a son of Horus.

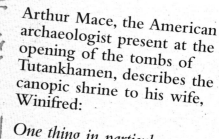

Arthur Mace, the American archaeologist present at the opening of the tombs of Tutankhamen, describes the canopic shrine to his wife, Winifred:

One thing in particular . . . simply knocked us all of a heap . . . I think it is the most beautiful thing I've ever seen anywhere. . . . Round [the canopic shrine] were four statues of goddesses, most un-Egyptian in attitude, and beautifully modelled. One simply couldn't take in what one saw; it was so wonderful we all came out dazed.

Nicholas Reeves,
The Complete Tutankhamen: The King, the Tomb, the Treasure

Inside the shrine

Within this giant shrine stood a canopic chest with four compartments. Tutankhamen's body parts were found inside these compartments rather than in the usual canopic jars. Each compartment had a stopper shaped like a human head. These represented Tutankhamen. Once the stoppers were removed, there were four golden coffinettes. These were smaller versions of the coffins in which Tutankhamen's mummy was found. The coffinettes contained the embalmed liver, lungs, stomach, and intestines of Tutankhamen.

THE ANUBIS SHRINE

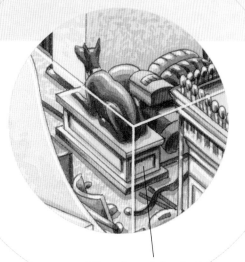

The Anubis shrine

As you enter the treasury, you'll see a striking black figure of a dog or jackal covered with linen. This is Anubis, carved from wood and coated in resin. He's sitting on a golden movable shrine and has a golden collar, piercing eyes, and upright ears—he seems to be guarding the treasury. He stares coldly back at you as you enter the room. Perhaps he looks angry because you're the first intruders for over 3,000 years!

The god of mummification

Anubis was the ancient Egyptian god of mummification. Embalming workshops were also called the Divine Halls of Anubis. The reason for removing the pharaoh's body parts was so that the embalmers could mummify the body. The body was dried out using a special type of salt before being washed and wiped dry. It was then wrapped in linen shrouds, with jewels and amulets placed in between each layer. Special resins then sealed each layer. The whole mummification process took 70 days.

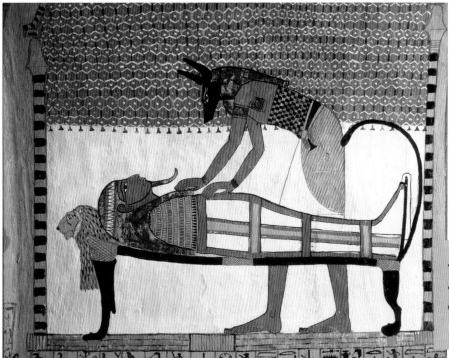

 EMBALMING PROCESS: SEE PAGE 26

A priest wearing the mask of Anubis attends the burial ceremony of a pharaoh.

The funeral

Scribes copied parts of the *Book of the Dead* onto rolls of papyrus (a type of paper) and placed them inside the tomb. The funeral procession began with priests and mourners following the king's coffin. Meanwhile, the tomb was filled with boxes, treasures, gifts, furniture, and food.

THE BOOK OF THE DEAD: SEE PAGE 23

Amulets, like this chlorite falcon, were placed inside the bandages of the mummy to protect it during the passage to the Afterlife. More than 150 jewels and amulets were discovered with Tutankhamen's mummy.

A passage from the *Book of the Dead*, an ancient Egyptian book that gave advice for a safe passage to the afterlife:

O lord of acacia trees! whose blooms are the first sensations, who binds the rags of mummies. This sad mortality! The boat is set upon its sledge and filled with yellow flowers. O jackal Anubis! I have passed through the underworld door. Nothing grows and nothing dies; all that was and would be, is. This life is a singular breath and your moving eye is time. . . .

www.jbeilharz.de/ellis/egypt.html

The Opening of the Mouth ceremony

When the coffin reached the tomb, the Opening of the Mouth ceremony was performed. A priest touched the mummy's mouth with a chisel and a special tool called an adze. Ancient Egyptians believed this ceremony allowed the mummy to eat, talk, and walk again. In many ancient Egyptian wall paintings, the priest who performs the Opening of the Mouth ceremony wears a mask of Anubis.

TIMELINE

1550–1070 BCE	**New Kingdom**
1550–1295 BCE	18th Dynasty
1352–1336 BCE	Akhenaten
1338–1336 BCE	Smenkhkare
1336–1327 BCE	Tutankhamen
1327–1323 BCE	Ay
1323–1295 BCE	Horemheb

All dates above are approximate reign dates.

1327 BCE **January–March**	Death of Tutankhamen, the mummy and tomb are prepared, funeral ceremony for Tutankhamen takes place, and the tomb is sealed.
c. 1319 BCE	Two separate robberies take place at Tutankhamen's tomb.
c. 1151–43 BCE	Workmen's huts are built over entrance of Tutankhamen's tomb, making it more difficult for archaeologists to find.
1922 November 4	Howard Carter discovers the entrance to Tutankhamen's tomb; over the following weeks he enters the antechamber, burial chamber, treasury, and annex.
1923 February 16	The burial chamber is opened.
1924 February 12	The sarcophagus lid is lifted.
1925 October	The lids of the outer coffins are removed to reveal the mummy of Tutankhamen.
1925 November	Autopsy of the mummy of Tutankhamen is started.
1930 November	Most of the objects in the tomb have been removed.

GLOSSARY

afterlife The place where the ancient Egyptians believed people went when they died.

amulets A magical charm or piece of jewelry that is supposed to protect the wearer from harm or evil.

Anubis The god of mummification, who watches over priests as they embalm dead bodies. In art, he is represented by a jackal or a man with a jackal's head.

archaeologists People who discover and examine old objects and buildings.

canopic jars Small jars that are used for storing the embalmed organs of a dead person.

coffinette Smaller versions of the coffins in which Tutankhamen's mummy was discovered. Coffinettes contained the internal organs of Tutankhamen.

dynasty A ruling family.

embalming Treating a dead body with salts to preserve it from decay.

faience A material that looks like glass and is made by heating powdered quartz. It is used to make cups, headrests, jewelry, and other ancient Egyptian artefacts.

flail A stick carried by a pharaoh, which symbolizes kingship and the fertility of the land.

funerary Describes objects that are used at a funeral.

gilt Covered in gold leaf (thin sheets of beaten gold).

Hathor Goddess of love, children, music, and dance. In pictures, she is usually shown as a cow.

hieroglyphs Pictures or symbols that represent words or sounds that are used in ancient Egyptian writing.

Horus The ancient Egyptian sky god, who often takes the form of a falcon. Also the son of Osiris and Isis. Often associated with Re, the sun god.

Isis Probably the greatest ancient Egyptian goddess. She was the mother of Horus and is the giver of life and guardian of children.

ivory The creamy white substance from elephant tusks that was used to make precious objects.

loincloth A piece of cloth that is worn around the hips and covers the private parts of the wearer.

Neith The goddess of war, also the protector of the stomach of the dead.

Nephthys Goddess of the dead, companion of the deceased, and comforter of mourners.

Osiris Husband and brother of Isis; later the god of underworld. In art, he appears in human form with a crown of reeds and ostrich feathers, carrying a scepter and flail.

resin A type of glue or gum.

rituals A set of actions that is performed during a religious ceremony.

sarcophagus A stone or wooden coffin covered in inscriptions. The name means "flesh eating."

scepter A king's staff.

scribes People who are employed to write.

Selkis Goddess of childbirth and protector of the intestines of the dead.

shabti A small statue, placed inside an ancient Egyptian tomb, to do the work of the dead person in the afterlife.

shrine A holy place, often where the image of a god is kept.

signet ring A ring with a seal bearing a person's initials or name on it.

telegram A written message that is sent by radio or electric signals. In the past, it was the best way of sending a message quickly.

FURTHER INFORMATION

Books

MacDonald, Alan. *Tutankhamen's Tomb*. Scholastic, 2004.

Morely, Jacqueline. *Inside the Tomb of Tutankhamen*. Enchanted Lion Books, 2005.

Murdoch, David. *Tutankhamen: The Life and Death of a Pharaoh*. Dorling Kindersley, 1998.

Websites

www.nationalgeographic.com/egypt/
Experience the drama of discovering the tomb with this exciting website from National Geographic.

www.touregypt.net/featurestories/tutt.htm
The story of Tutankhamen's life and the discovery of his tomb, with lots of photographs of artefacts from the tomb.

www.geocities.com/athens/delphi/3499/ TUTSHOME.HTM
Take a virtual tour of Tutankhamen's tomb and see the objects discovered in each chamber.

www.bbc.co.uk/history/ancient/egyptians/ tutankhamen_gallery.shtml
A gallery of photographs showing some of the most beautiful objects discovered in Tutankhamen's tomb.

INDEX

Page numbers in **bold** refer to illustrations.

afterlife **5**, 6, 11, 12, 14, 16, 17, 18, 19, 22, 23, 24, 25, 26, 29, 31
annex **5**, 14, **14**, 15, 16
antechamber **5**, 10, **10**, 11, 12, 14, 18
Anubis shrine **5**, 28, **28**

Book of Amduat 19
Book of the Dead 18, 19, 23, 25, 29
Book of the Heavenly Cow 19
burial chamber **5**, 6, 13, 18, **18**, 19, **19**, 24, 30

Callender, A. R. **18**
canopic jar 27, **27**
canopic shrine **5**, 26, **26**, 27
Carnarvon, Lord 5, 9
Carter, Howard 5, 7, 8, 9, 10, 11, 13, 14, **14**, 15, 18, **18**, 21, 23, 26, 30
cartouche 8
coffin **5**, 6, 20, **20**, 21, **21**, 22, 25, 27, 29
couches 10, 11, **11**, 12

Dwat 25

funeral boats 25, **25**
funerary beds 11, 14, **14**

goddesses and gods
    Ammut 11

Amun 7, **7**
Anubis **12**, 19, 28, **28**, 29, 31
Duamutef 27
Hathor 24, 31
Horus 27, 31
Isis 19, 20, 26
Mehet 11
Mehet-Weret 11
Neith 20, 26, 31
Nephthys 20, 26
Osiris 19, 20, 23, 31
Selkis 20, 26, **26**, 31
Shu 15
golden mask 22, **22**
guardian statues **5**, 11, 12, **12**, 13

headrests 15, **15**
hieroglyphs 9, 31

ka 13
Karnak 7

Luxor 4, 5

Mace, Arthur 27
mummification 6, 12, **12**, 13, 26, 28, **28**
mummy 20, 22, **22**, 23, 25, 27, 29, 30

New Kingdom 4, 7, 17, 25
Nile, River 4, 11

Old Kingdom 4, 7
Opening of the Mouth ceremony, the 19, 29

pharaohs 4, 6, 7, 8, 9, 10, 13, 14, 15, 16, 17, 21, 22, 25, 27, 28
    Akhenaten 7
    Ankhesenamun 12, **13**
    Ay 7
    Horemheb 7
    Rameses II 9
    Rameses VI 4
    Tutankhamen 4, 5, 7, 8, 9, 10, 11, 12, 13, **13**, 14, 15, 16, 17, 18, 19, 20, 21, 22, **22**, 23, **23**, 24, 25, 26, 27, 30, 31
pyramids 4, 7

religion 11, 17

sarcophagus **5**, 6, 20, **20**, 30, 31
seals 8, 9, **9**
Senet 17, **17**
shabti 24, **24**, 25
shrine 18, 19

Thebes 5, 7
tomb 4, 5, 6, **6**, 7, 8, 9, 10, 11, 14, **14**, 16, 17, 19, 25, 29, 30
tomb robbers 6, 7, 8, 14, 16, 24
treasure 6, **8**, 10, 13, 29
treasury 24, **24**

Valley of the Kings 4, **4**, 5, 10, 19